April 2012

U.S. POSTAL SERVICE

Mail Processing Network Exceeds What Is Needed for Declining Mail Volume

G A O

Accountability * Integrity * Reliability

GAO-12-470

Highlights

Highlights of GAO-12-470, a report to congressional requesters

U.S. POSTAL SERVICE

Mail Processing Network Exceeds What Is Needed for Declining Mail Volume

Why GAO Did This Study

Since 2006, the U.S. Postal Service has taken actions to reduce its excess capacity. Such actions have made progress toward consolidating the mail processing network to increase efficiency and reduce costs while meeting delivery standards. However, since 2006, the gap between USPS expenses and revenues has grown significantly. In February 2012, USPS projected that its net losses would reach $21 billion by 2016.

As requested, this report addresses (1) actions USPS has taken since 2006 to reduce excess capacity—in facilities, staff, equipment, and transportation; (2) USPS plans to consolidate its mail processing network; and (3) key stakeholder issues and challenges related to USPS's plans. GAO reviewed relevant documents and data, interviewed USPS officials, reviewed proposed legislation, and reviewed stakeholder comments to USPS plans for changing delivery service standards.

What GAO Recommends

GAO is not making new recommendations in this report, as it has previously reported to Congress on the urgent need for a comprehensive package of actions to improve USPS's financial viability and has provided Congress with strategies and options to consider. USPS had no comments on a draft of this report.

View GAO-12-470. For more information, contact Lorelei St. James at (202) 512-2834 or stjamesl@gao.gov.

What GAO Found

Since 2006, the U.S. Postal Service (USPS) has closed redundant facilities and consolidated mail processing operations and transportation to reduce excess capacity in its network, resulting in reported cost savings of about $2.4 billion. Excess capacity remains, however, because of continuing and accelerating declines in First-Class Mail volume, automation improvements that sort mail faster and more efficiently, and increasing mail preparation and transportation by business mailers, much of whose mail now bypasses most of USPS's processing network.

In December 2011, USPS issued a proposal for consolidating its mail processing network, which is based on proposed changes to overnight delivery service standards for First-Class Mail and Periodicals. Consolidating its network is one of several initiatives, including moving from a 6-day to a 5-day delivery schedule and reducing compensation and benefits, that USPS has proposed to meet a savings goal of $22.5 billion by 2016. This goal includes saving $4 billion by consolidating its mail processing and transportation network and reducing excess capacity as indicated in the table below. The Postal Regulatory Commission is currently reviewing USPS's proposal to change delivery service standards.

2011 USPS Estimate of Mail Processing Excess Capacity to Be Eliminated by Proposed Changes in First-Class and Periodical Delivery Standards

	2011 processing network	Excess capacity
Facilities	461 processing facilities	223 processing facilities
Workforce	154,325 positions	Up to 35,000 positions
Equipment	About 8,000 pieces of mail processing equipment	3,000 pieces of mail processing equipment
Transportation	1.5 billion trips between processing facilities	376 million trips between processing facilities

Source: USPS.

Stakeholder issues and other challenges could prevent USPS from implementing its plan for consolidating its mail processing network or achieving its cost savings goals. Although some business mailers and Members of Congress have expressed support for consolidating mail processing facilities, other mailers, Members of Congress, affected communities, and employee organizations have raised issues. Key issues raised by business mailers are that closing facilities could increase their transportation costs and decrease service. Employee associations are concerned that reducing service could result in a greater loss of mail volume and revenue that could worsen USPS's financial condition. USPS has said that given its huge deficits, capturing cost savings wherever possible will be vital. USPS has asked Congress to address its challenges, and Congress is considering legislation that would include different approaches to addressing USPS's financial problems. A bill originating in the Senate provides for employee buyouts but delays moving to 5-day delivery, while a House bill creates a commission to make operational decisions such as facility closures and permits USPS to reduce delivery days. If Congress prefers to retain the current delivery service standards and associated network, decisions will need to be made about how USPS's costs for providing these services will be paid, including additional cost reductions or revenue sources.

_____ United States Government Accountability Office

Contents

Abbreviations

AMP	Area Mail Processing
BRAC	Base Realignment and Closure
DPS	Delivery Point Sequencing
OIG	Office of Inspector General
PAEA	Postal Accountability and Enhancement Act
PRC	Postal Regulatory Commission
USPS	U.S. Postal Service

This is a work of the U.S. government and is not subject to copyright protection in the United States. The published product may be reproduced and distributed in its entirety without further permission from GAO. However, because this work may contain copyrighted images or other material, permission from the copyright holder may be necessary if you wish to reproduce this material separately.

United States Government Accountability Office
Washington, DC 20548

April 12, 2012

The Honorable Susan M. Collins
Ranking Member
Committee on Homeland Security and Governmental Affairs
United States Senate

The Honorable Thomas R. Carper
Chairman
Subcommittee on Federal Financial Management, Government
 Information, Federal Services, and International Security
Committee on Homeland Security and Governmental Affairs
United States Senate

The Honorable Darrell E. Issa
Chairman
Committee on Oversight and Government Reform
House of Representatives

The U.S. Postal Service's (USPS) dire financial situation has increased the urgency for agreement on an effective strategy to better align USPS's postal services with its costs and revenues. USPS has noted that the decline in First-Class Mail volume accelerated more than expected and predicted that volume will continue to fall. By fiscal year 2020, USPS expects to lose over 60 percent of the First-Class Mail volume that it had in fiscal year 2006.[1] Declining First-Class Mail volumes, development of automated mail processing equipment, and "workshare" initiatives (e.g., mailers applying bar codes, presorting the mail, and entering mail into the postal network closer to its final delivery point) have led to a mail processing network—including postal facilities, staff, equipment, and transportation resources—that is larger than needed to process and distribute current and projected levels of mail.

---

[1]Mail that is processed in USPS's network includes two broad categories: market-dominant and competitive. Market-dominant products primarily include First-Class Mail (e.g., correspondence, bills, payments, and statements), Standard Mail (mainly bulk advertising and direct mail solicitations), Periodicals (mainly magazines and local newspapers), and some types of Package Services (primarily single-piece Parcel Post, Media Mail, library mail, and bound printed matter). Market-dominant mail and services represent about 86 percent of USPS's revenue. Competitive mail refers to Priority Mail and Express Mail that compete with delivery services offered by private businesses.

Over the past decade, USPS has taken steps to reduce its excess capacity to move toward optimizing its mail processing network—one where processing facilities are located to maximize revenues, increase efficiency, and minimize costs while meeting delivery standards. Since 2006, the gap between USPS expenses and revenues has grown significantly (see fig. 1). At the end of fiscal year 2011, USPS had a net loss of $5.1 billion and $2 billion remaining on its $15 billion statutory borrowing limit.[2] In February 2012, USPS issued a 5-year plan that projected its net loss to increase to over $21 billion by 2016 and set a goal to reduce annual costs by at least $22.5 billion by 2016. The Postmaster General has stated that maintaining a vast national postal infrastructure is no longer realistic. We have testified that USPS cannot continue providing services at current levels without dramatic changes in its cost structure.[3] Optimizing USPS's mail processing network would help USPS by bringing down costs related to excess and inefficient network resources.

Figure 1: USPS Net Operating Profit and Loss, Fiscal Years 2006 to 2011

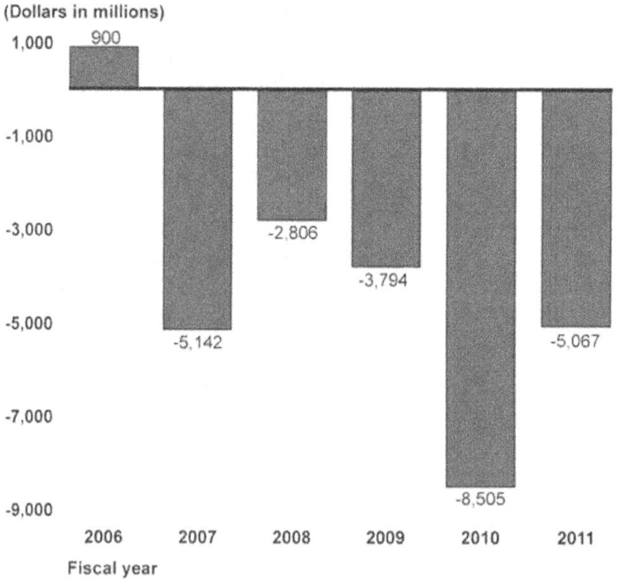

(Dollars in millions)

Fiscal year

Source: USPS.

[2]39 U.S.C. § 2005(a)(2).

[3]GAO, *U.S. Postal Service: Actions Needed to Stave Off Financial Insolvency*, GAO-11-926T (Washington, D.C.: Sept. 6, 2011).

You requested that we study opportunities for USPS to reduce excess capacity in its mail processing network. This report addresses (1) past actions USPS has taken to reduce excess capacity, (2) USPS's plan to consolidate its mail processing network, and (3) key stakeholder issues and challenges USPS faces in consolidating its mail processing network.

To describe what actions USPS has taken to reduce excess capacity and its reported results of these actions, we obtained data from USPS related to changes in its mail processing network, workforce, and costs as well as an updated forecast for First-Class Mail volume to 2020. To calculate the 5-year cost savings that USPS achieved, we took the difference of the network costs for fiscal years 2006 and 2011 that USPS reported to us. We also obtained data from USPS and USPS Office of Inspector General (OIG) reports regarding cost savings related to USPS initiatives to reduce excess capacity. Further, we reviewed USPS annual reports to Congress and its network plans as section 302 of the Postal Accountability and Enhancement Act of 2006 requires USPS to submit; related GAO and USPS OIG reports; as well as other relevant studies relating to reducing excess capacity in USPS's mail processing network. To examine USPS's future plans to consolidate its mail processing network, we reviewed USPS's December 2011 plan to change delivery service standards and consolidate its mail processing network by reducing facilities, staff, equipment, and transportation resources. We also reviewed USPS's 5-year business plan to profitability issued in February 2012. We interviewed USPS senior management and local facility mangers in Illinois about the current processing network and future plans for that network. We also reviewed documents in the ongoing Postal Regulatory Commission (PRC) proceeding of USPS's proposed changes in service standards and its plan for consolidating its mail processing network. PRC is reviewing USPS's estimated cost savings, service impacts, and public input on the network consolidation plan and expects to complete its review sometime after July 2012.

To determine key issues and challenges USPS officials face in consolidating its mail processing network, we reviewed and summarized concerns from postal stakeholders responding to USPS's September 2011 *Federal Register* notice on its proposed changes to service standards for First-Class Mail, Periodicals, and Standard Mail. We also interviewed USPS officials, and reviewed stakeholder testimonies and published letters from Members of Congress commenting on USPS plans to change delivery service standards and close facilities. Further, we reviewed pending legislative proposals that could affect USPS's efforts to address excess capacity and consolidate its mail processing network. For more information on our scope and methodology, see appendix I.

We conducted this performance audit from April 2011 through April 2012 in accordance with generally accepted government auditing standards. Those standards require that we plan and perform the audit to obtain sufficient, appropriate evidence to provide a reasonable basis for our findings and conclusions based on our audit objectives. We believe that the evidence obtained provides a reasonable basis for our findings and conclusions based on our audit objectives.

Background

USPS has a vast mail processing network consisting of multiple facilities with different functions, as shown in figure 2. In fiscal year 2011, according to USPS, it had a nationwide mail processing network that included 461 facilities, 154,325 full-time employees, and about 8,000 pieces of mail processing equipment. This network transports mail from where it is entered into USPS's network, sorts it for carriers to deliver, and distributes it to a location near its destination in accordance with specific delivery standards. USPS receives mail into its processing network from different sources such as mail carriers, post offices, and commercial entities. Once USPS receives mail from the public and commercial entities, it uses automated equipment to sort and prepare mail for distribution. The mail is then transported between processing facilities where it will be further processed for mail carriers to pick up for delivery.

Figure 2: Mail Flow through the National Infrastructure

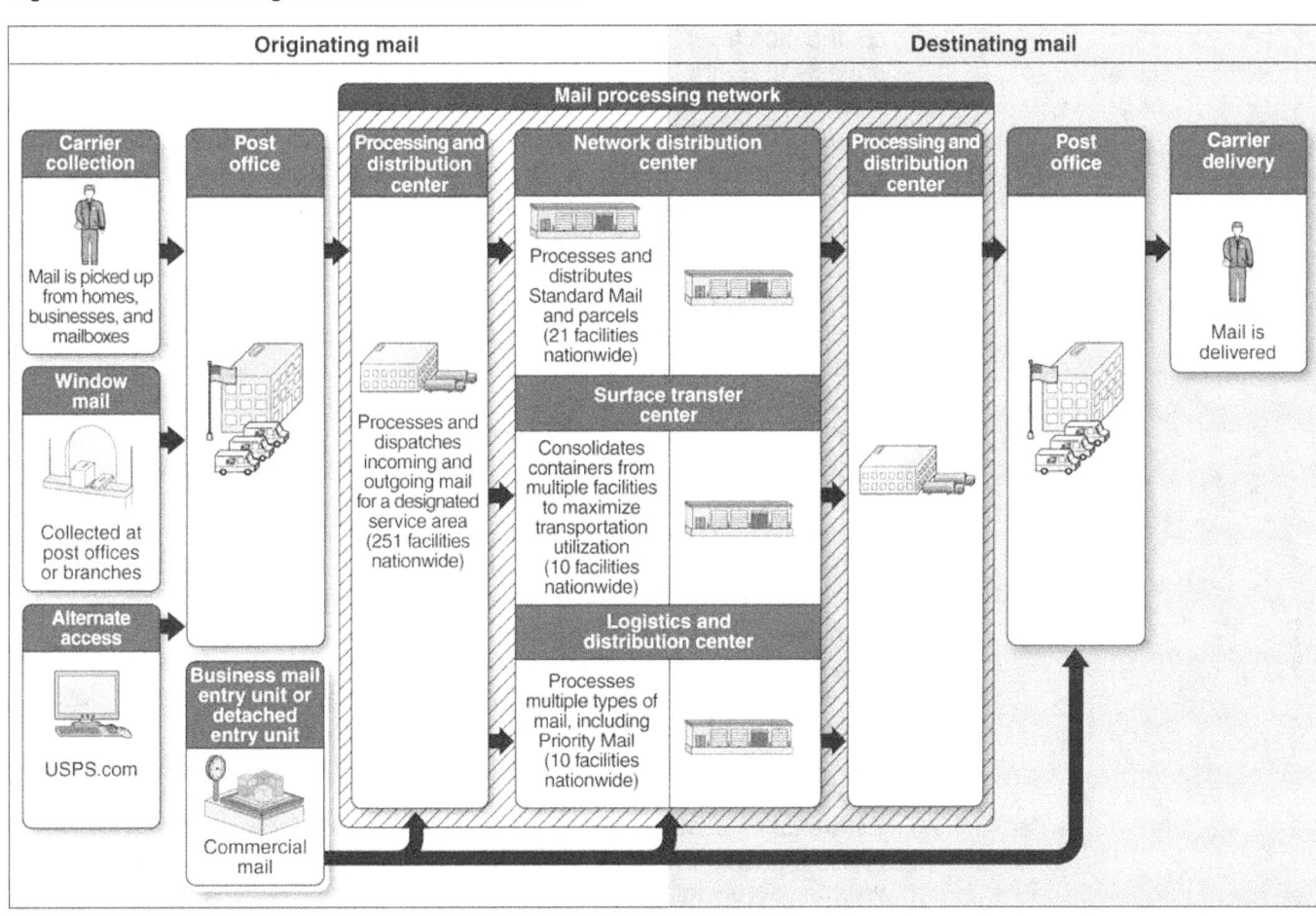

Sources: GAO and USPS.

Note: Originating mail refers to outgoing and local mail that enters the point of origin for mail processing. Local mail remains within the facility and is combined with destinating mail from other origin facilities. Destinating mail refers to mail arriving at the point of entry for distribution and dispatch to a post office for delivery. Some mail moves from one Processing Distribution Center to another without going through the Network Distribution Center, Surface Transfer Center, or Logistics and Distribution Center.

Trends in mail use underscore the need for fundamental changes to USPS's business model. First-Class Mail volume peaked in fiscal year 2001 at nearly 104 billion pieces and has fallen about 29 percent, or 30 billion pieces, as of fiscal year 2011. Although First-Class Mail volume accounted for 44 percent of total mail volume in fiscal year 2011, it generated about 49 percent of USPS's revenue. In comparison, Standard Mail (primarily advertising) accounted for 51 percent of total mail volume but generated only about 27 percent of USPS's revenue. Further, it takes about three pieces of Standard Mail, on average, to equal the financial contribution from one piece of First-Class Mail. Looking forward, USPS projects that First-Class Mail will decline significantly between now and 2020. For the first time, in 2010, less than 50 percent of all bills were paid by mail as consumers continue to switch to electronic alternatives. USPS projects that Standard Mail volume will remain roughly flat between now and 2020, thereby increasing its share of revenues generated. Almost 60 percent of mail received by households in 2010 was advertising.

USPS has said that its mail processing network is configured primarily so that it can meet the First-Class Mail delivery standards within a 1- to 5-day window, depending on where the mail is entered into the postal system and where it will be delivered. Most First-Class Mail is to be delivered in 1 day when it is sent within the local area served by the destinating mail processing center; 2 days when it is sent within reasonable driving distance, which USPS considers within a 12-hour drive time; 3 days for other mail, such as mail transported over long distances by air; and 4 to 5 days if delivery is from the 48 contiguous states to the noncontiguous states, Puerto Rico, the U.S. Virgin Islands, or Guam. Delivery service standards within the contiguous 48 states generally range from 1 to 10 days for other types of mail. Delivery service standards help USPS, mailers, and customers set realistic expectations for the number of days mail takes to be delivered, and to plan their activities accordingly. USPS requires a certain level of facilities, staff, equipment, and transportation resources to consistently meet First-Class Mail and other delivery service standards as expected by its customers. The USPS processing and transportation networks were developed during a time of growing mail volume, largely to achieve service standards for First-Class Mail and Periodicals, particularly the overnight service standards.

To revise service standards, USPS can propose changes, such as elimination of overnight delivery for First-Class Mail, through a regulatory proceeding that includes the consideration of public comments.[4] Further,

---

[4]The Postal Accountability and Enhancement Act of 2006 (PAEA) required USPS to establish a set of modern service standards for its market-dominant products by regulation in consultation with PRC. Pub. L. No. 109-435, § 301 (Dec. 20, 2006). Once these standards were established, PAEA directed USPS to begin to measure and publicly report on its service performance for all market-dominant products. In December 2007, USPS finalized regulations establishing service standards for market-dominant products. 72 Fed. Reg. 72216 (Dec. 19, 2007).

whenever USPS proposes a change in the nature of postal services that affects service on a nationwide basis, USPS must request an advisory opinion on the change from PRC.[5] In addition, USPS annual appropriations have mandated 6-day delivery and rural mail delivery at certain levels.[6] USPS has asked Congress to allow it to change the delivery standard from 6- to 5-day-a-week delivery.

USPS and other stakeholders have long recognized the need for USPS to reduce excess capacity in its mail processing network.

- In 2002, USPS released a *Transformation Plan* that provided a comprehensive strategy to adapt the mail processing and delivery networks to changing customer demands, eroding mail volumes, and rising costs.[7] One key goal cited in the plan was for USPS to become more efficient by standardizing operations and reducing excess capacity in its mail processing and distribution infrastructure.

- In 2003, a presidential commission examining USPS's future issued a report recommending several actions that would facilitate USPS efforts to consolidate its mail processing network.[8] The commission determined that USPS had far more facilities than it needed and those facilities that it did require often were not used in the most efficient manner. The commission recommended that Congress create a Postal Network Optimization Commission modeled in part on the Department of Defense's Base Realignment and Closure (BRAC) Commission, to make recommendations relating to the consolidation and rationalization of USPS's mail processing and distribution infrastructure. We reported in 2010 that Congress has considered BRAC-type approaches to assist in restructuring organizations that are facing key financial challenges.[9] These commissions have gained

---

[5]39 U.S.C. § 3661(b).

[6]These provisions have specified that "6-day delivery and rural delivery of mail shall continue at not less than the 1983 level." See, e.g., Pub. L. No. 112-74, 125 Stat. 786 (Dec. 23, 2011).

[7]USPS, *United States Postal Service Transformation Plan* (April 2002).

[8]President's Commission on the United States Postal Service, *Embracing the Future: Making the Tough Choices to Preserve Universal Mail Service* (Washington, D.C.: July 31, 2003).

[9]GAO, *U.S. Postal Service: Strategies and Options to Facilitate Progress toward Financial Viability*, GAO-10-455 (Washington, D.C.: Apr. 12, 2010).

consensus and developed proposed legislative or other changes to address difficult public policy issues. The 2003 presidential commission also recommended that USPS exercise discipline in its hiring practices to "rightsize" and realign its workforce with minimal displacement.

- The Postal Accountability and Enhancement Act (PAEA), enacted in 2006, encouraged USPS to expeditiously move forward in its streamlining efforts and required USPS to develop a network plan describing its long-term vision for rationalizing its infrastructure and workforce. The plan was to include a strategy to consolidate its mail processing network by eliminating excess capacity and identifying cost savings.[10] In June 2008, USPS provided its Network Plan to Congress, which we describe in more detail later in the report.

- In 2009, GAO added USPS to its list of high-risk areas needing attention by Congress and the executive branch to achieve broad-based transformation.[11] Given the decline in mail volume and revenue, we suggested that USPS develop and implement a broad restructuring plan—with input from PRC and other stakeholders and approval by Congress and the administration. We added that this plan should address how USPS plans to realign postal services (such as delivery frequency and delivery standards); better align its costs and revenues; optimize its operations, network, and workforce; increase mail volume and revenue; and retain earnings so that it can finance needed capital investments and repay its growing debt. In 2009, we testified that maintaining USPS's financial viability as the provider of affordable, high-quality universal postal services would require actions in a number of areas, such as rightsizing its retail and mail processing networks by consolidating operations and closing unnecessary facilities.[12] Furthermore, in 2010 we provided strategies and options that Congress could consider to better align USPS costs with revenues and address constraints and legal restrictions that limit USPS's ability to reduce costs and improve efficiency.[13] We reported

---

[10]Pub. L. No. 109-435, § 302.

[11]GAO, *High-Risk Series: Restructuring the U.S. Postal Service to Achieve Sustainable Financial Viability,* GAO-09-937SP (Washington, D.C.: July 2009).

[12]GAO, *U.S. Postal Service: Network Rightsizing Needed to Help Keep USPS Financially Viable,* GAO-09-674T (Washington, D.C.: May 20, 2009).

[13]GAO-10-455.

that USPS could close major mail processing facilities and relax delivery standards to facilitate consolidations and closures of mail processing facilities as options for reducing network costs.

Past Actions to Reduce Excess Capacity

From fiscal years 2006 through 2011, USPS data showed that it reduced mail processing and transportation costs by $2.4 billion—or 16 percent— by reducing the number of mail processing work hours, facilities, and employees as shown in table 1. Specifically, USPS data show that it eliminated about 35 percent of its total mail processing work hours, 32 percent of its mail processing facilities, and 20 percent of its full-time mail processing employees.

Table 1: Reported Decrease in Mail Processing Work Hours, Facilities, Employees, and Costs, from Fiscal Years 2006 to 2011

	2006	2011	Change from 2006 to 2011	Percentage change from 2006 to 2011
Mail processing work hours (thousands)	332,269	215,283	-116,986	-35
Facilities	673	461	-212	-32
Full-time employees	192,411	154,325	-38,086	-20
Mail processing and transportation-related costs[a] (dollars in billions)	$15.6	$13.2	-$2.4	-16

Source: USPS data.

[a]Mail processing costs include facility-, employee-, and transportation-related expenses.

Although most of USPS's cost savings during fiscal years 2006 through 2011 came from reducing its work hours and workforce, USPS also took some actions to consolidate or close facilities and realign its transportation network. During this period, USPS reported that it focused on three core initiatives that together saved about $414 million.[14]

---

[14]USPS is required to prepare and submit to Congress a report on how postal decisions have affected or will affect its rationalization plans no later than 90 days after the end of each fiscal year. Pub. L. No. 109-435, § 302(c)(4) (Dec. 20, 2006). USPS has submitted these annual reports for fiscal years 2008 through 2011.

- *Closed excess Remote Encoding Centers and Airport Mail Centers:* USPS established Remote Encoding Centers to apply address bar codes to letters that the automated equipment in mail processing plants could not read. As automated equipment improved, USPS relied less on Remote Encoding Centers. In fiscal year 2006, USPS reported that it had 12 Remote Encoding Centers, but only 2 by fiscal year 2011, resulting in savings of $10.3 million.[15] USPS established Airport Mail Centers to expedite the transfer of mail to and from commercial air carriers. Excess capacity existed in these facilities because of declining mail volumes and because USPS transferred some mail from air transportation to its surface transportation network. To reduce excess capacity, USPS began transferring Airport Mail Center operations to processing and distribution facilities. This enabled USPS to reduce costs at Airport Mail Centers by closing or outsourcing operations and repurposing facilities. In fiscal year 2006, USPS reported that it had 77 Airport Mail Centers, but only 1 remains. These closures resulted in savings of $108 million according to USPS.

- *Consolidated Area Mail Processing (AMP) operations*: According to a January 2012, USPS OIG report, USPS used its AMP study process to complete 100 consolidations from fiscal years 2006 through 2011.[16] An AMP study examines the feasibility of consolidating some mail processing operations from one or more postal facilities to other facilities to improve operational efficiency. An AMP study that has been implemented may involve consolidating origination mail, or destinating mail, or both, to increase mail processing efficiency and reduce excess capacity on equipment, facilities, and work hours. USPS officials at headquarters used a nationwide model to identify opportunities for consolidating operations and used input from local area and district officials for an in-depth analysis of the feasibility of such consolidations, which informed the final decision on whether or

[15]Data from USPS fiscal year 2006 and 2011 annual reports.

[16]USPS's OIG report determined that a valid business case existed for 31 of the 32 implemented AMP studies (97 percent) reviewed, and that those cases were supported by adequate capacity, increased efficiency, reduced work hours, and mail processing costs, and improved service standards. United States Postal Service, Office of Inspector General, *U.S. Postal Service Past Network Optimization Initiatives,* CI-AR-12-003 (Arlington, VA: Jan. 9, 2012).

not to approve the AMP study.[17] According to USPS data, it achieved savings of $167 million from AMP consolidations in fiscal years 2010 and 2011.

- *Transformed the Bulk Mail Center network*: In the past, mailers dropped their bulk mail at a network of 21 Bulk Mail Centers. USPS would then process and transport the bulk mail to its final destinations. By 2007, however, a significant portion of this mail bypassed the Bulk Mail Center network and was dropped at a processing plant closer to its final delivery point. In fiscal year 2009, USPS reported that it had begun transforming its 21 Bulk Mail Centers into Network Distribution Centers and completed the transformation in fiscal year 2010.[18] According to USPS, this was designed to better align work hours with workload and improve transportation utilization, resulting in cost savings of $129 million.

Even after taking these actions to reduce excess capacity, USPS stated that excess capacity continues and structural changes are necessary to eliminate it. Three major reasons for continued excess capacity include the following:

- *Accelerating declines in mail volume*: Since 2006, declines in mail volume have continued to worsen. For example, single-piece First-Class Mail has dropped by almost 19 billion pieces. Furthermore, USPS's volume forecasts to 2020 indicate that the decline in First-Class Mail volume will not abate going forward but instead will continue—from 73 billion pieces in 2011 to 39 billion pieces in 2020—further exacerbating the problem of costly excess capacity (see fig. 3). Declining First-Class Mail volume is primarily attributed to the increasing number of electronic communications and transactions. The recent recession and other economic difficulties have further accelerated mail volume decline.

---

[17] In 2010, we analyzed 32 AMP studies that were implemented, approved, or not approved since the beginning of fiscal year 2009, and determined that USPS had followed its realignment guidance by completing each step of the process and consistently applying its criteria in its reviews. GAO, *Mail Processing Network Initiatives Progressing, and Guidance for Consolidating Area Mail Processing Operations Being Followed*, GAO-10-731 (Washington, D.C.: June 16, 2010).

[18] United States Postal Service, *Meeting the Challenge: The Power of the Mail,* fiscal year 2009 annual report.

Figure 3: USPS First-Class Mail Volume Data and Forecast, Billions of Pieces, Fiscal Years 2010-2020

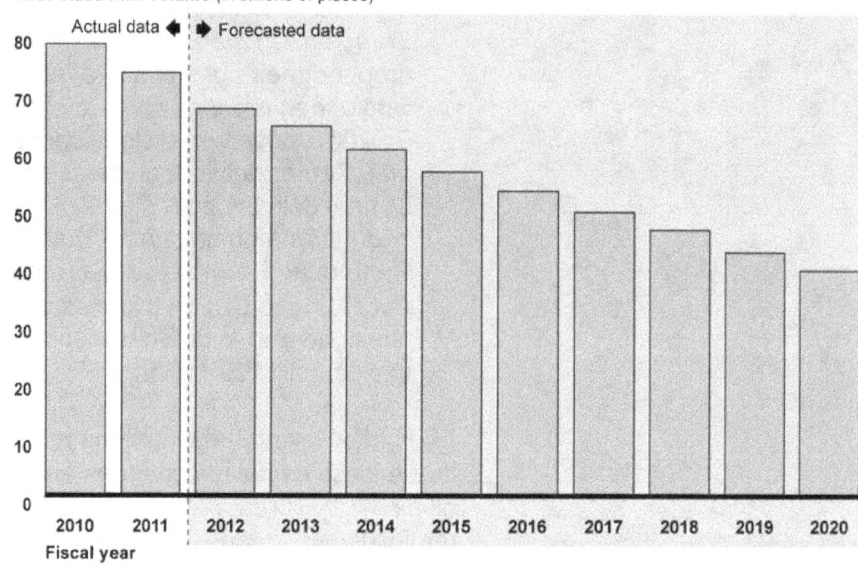

First-Class mail volume (in billions of pieces)

Source: GAO analysis of USPS data.

- *Continuing automation improvements*: These improvements have enabled USPS to sort mail faster and more efficiently. For example, USPS's Flats Sequencing System machines automatically sort larger mail pieces (e.g., magazines and catalogs) into the order that they will be delivered. At the end of fiscal year 2011, USPS reported that it had deployed 100 flats sequencing machines to 46 sites and the Flats Sequencing System covered nearly 43,000 delivery routes and processed an average of almost 60 percent of flats at more than half of those sites.

- *Increasing mail preparation and transportation by mailers*: While most First-Class Mail goes through USPS's entire mail processing network, around 83 percent of Standard Mail is destination entered—that is, business mailers enter mail within a local area where it will be delivered, bypassing most of USPS's mail processing network and long-distance transportation.[19] The percentage of mail that is destination entered has increased 16 percent over the last decade.

USPS Plan to Consolidate Its Mail Processing Network

On December 15, 2011, USPS asked PRC to review and provide an advisory opinion on its proposal to change its delivery service standards, primarily by changing its delivery standards to eliminate overnight delivery service for most First-Class Mail and Periodicals.[20] USPS has stated that these changes in delivery service standards are a necessary part of its plan to consolidate its mail processing operations, workforce, and facilities. Under this plan, the 42 percent of First-Class Mail that is currently delivered within 1 day would be delivered within 2 to 3 days. See table 2 for the percentage of First-Class Mail volume that is intended to be delivered within the current and proposed delivery service standards.

Table 2: Proportion of First-Class Mail Volume by Delivery Service Standard as Proposed by USPS

Service standard	Current percentage	Proposed percentage
1-day	42	0
2-day	27	51
3-day	32	49
4-day	0.3	0.3

Source: USPS.

Note: Totals do not add to 100 percent because of rounding.

USPS's plan included details on facilities, staff, equipment, and transportation that USPS would eliminate as a result of the change in delivery service standards and the estimated cost savings from these changes. On the basis of an analysis of fiscal year 2010 costs, USPS estimated that service standard changes centered on eliminating overnight service for significant portions of First-Class Mail and

---

[19]Mail that is destination entered is sorted and transported by mailers to USPS facilities that are generally closer to the final destination where the mail will be delivered.

[20]Whenever USPS proposes a change in the nature of postal services that affects service on a nationwide basis, USPS must request a nonbinding advisory opinion on the change from PRC. 39 U.S.C. § 3661(b). First-Class Mail and Periodicals that meet specified mail preparation requirements and originate and destinate within designated areas may still be eligible for overnight service.

Periodicals could save approximately $2 billion annually when fully implemented. To save this amount, USPS stated that it plans to use the already established AMP study process, which was designed to achieve cost savings through the consolidation of operations and facilities with excess capacity. USPS has stated that the AMP process provides opportunities for USPS to reduce costs, improve service, and operate as a leaner, more efficient organization by making better use of resources, space, staffing, processing equipment, and transportation. In a February 2012 press release, USPS announced that it would begin consolidating or closing 223 processing facilities during the summer and fall of 2012—contingent on a final decision to change service standards, which it said it expects to complete sometime in March.[21] USPS added that it will not close any facilities prior to May 15, 2012, as agreed upon with some Members of Congress. PRC is currently reviewing the details of USPS's proposal to revise service standards, the estimated cost savings, the potential impacts on both senders and recipients, and USPS's justification for the change to advise USPS and Congress on the merits of USPS's proposal. PRC procedures enable interested stakeholders, including the public, to file questions and comments to PRC regarding USPS's proposal.[22] PRC expects to issue its advisory opinion on USPS's proposal after the time for obtaining public input is concluded in July 2012.

USPS has stated that consolidating its networks is unachievable without relaxing delivery service standards. The Postmaster General testified last September that such a change would allow for a longer operating window to process mail, which would enable USPS to reduce unneeded facilities, work hours, workforce positions, and equipment. USPS identified scenarios looking at how constraints within the mail processing network affected excess capacity and found that if the current standard for overnight First-Class Mail service was relaxed, plant consolidation could occur, which would more fully maximize the use of facilities, labor, and equipment. USPS estimates of excess capacity it wants to eliminate based on proposed changes to its overnight delivery service standards are shown in table 3.

---

[21]USPS's website lists these specific processing facilities. See http://about.usps.com/what-we-are-doing/our-future-network/assets/pdf/communications-list-022212.pdf.

[22]Since PRC is examining USPS's proposal and cost estimates for revising its delivery service standards, we did not assess the reliability of USPS's database used for estimating the cost savings.

Table 3: 2011 USPS Estimate of Mail Processing Excess Capacity Based on Proposed Changes in First-Class and Periodical Delivery Standards

Processing network element	2011 network	Excess capacity
Facilities	461 processing facilities	223 processing facilities
Workforce	154,325 positions	Up to 35,000 positions
Equipment	About 8,000 pieces of mail processing equipment	3,000 pieces of mail processing equipment
Transportation	1.5 billion trips between processing facilities	376 million trips between processing facilities

Source: USPS.

Facilities and Workforce

USPS estimated that it could consolidate, all or in part, 223 processing facilities based on its proposed changes in First-Class and Periodical delivery service standards. USPS has also specified that changing delivery service standards would enable it to remove up to 35,000 mail processing positions as it consolidates operations into fewer facilities. The number of employees per facility ranges from 50 to 2,000. Reducing work hours and the size and cost of its workforce will be key for USPS, since its workforce generates about 80 percent of its costs. In addition, USPS entered into a collective bargaining agreement with the American Postal Workers Union in April 2011 that established a two-tier career pay schedule for new employees that is 10.2 percent lower than the existing pay schedule. This labor agreement also allowed USPS to increase its use of noncareer employees from 5.9 percent to 20 percent, thereby enabling USPS to hire more lower-paid noncareer employees when replacing full-time career employees.

Equipment

USPS has also pointed out that it has about 8,000 pieces of equipment used for processing mail, but could function with as few as 5,000 pieces if it adopts the proposed delivery service standards. Declining mail volume has resulted in a reduced need for machines that sort mail using Delivery Point Sequencing (DPS) programs, on a national level, by approximately one-half.[23] According to USPS, however, a reduction of Delivery Point Sequencing machinery use would allow for greater reliance on machinery that incurs lower maintenance costs. In addition, much of this equipment

---

[23]DPS enables USPS to sort the next day's destination letter- and flat-shaped mail pieces into the precise order in which they will be delivered on carrier routes. After mail is run through DPS, it is transported to delivery units, where carriers take it for delivery.

is currently used to sort mail only 4 to 6 hours per day. USPS plans to optimize the use of its remaining equipment to sort mail by increasing its maximum usage up to 20 hours per day.

Transportation

USPS estimates that it makes more transportation trips than are currently necessary. USPS's transportation network includes the movement of mail between origin and destination processing plants. USPS, however, has estimated that changing its delivery service standards as proposed in December 2011 would enable it to reduce these facility-to-facility trips by about 25 percent, or 376 million trips.

Relaxing delivery standards and consolidating its mail processing network is just one part of USPS's overall strategy to achieve financial stability. On the revenue side, USPS has noted that it cannot increase mail prices beyond the Consumer Price Index cap, and price increases cannot remedy the revenue loss resulting from First-Class Mail volume loss. USPS has also reported that it faces restrictions on entering new lines of business and does not see any revenue growth solution to its current financial problems. In February 2012, USPS announced a 5-year business plan to achieve financial stability that included a goal of achieving $22.5 billion in annual cost savings by the end of fiscal year 2016. USPS's proposed changes in its mail processing and transportation networks are included in its 5-year business plan, as are initiatives to save

1. $9 billion in network operations, of which $4 billion would come from consolidating its mail processing and transportation networks;

2. $5 billion in compensation and benefits; and

3. $8.5 billion through legislative changes, such as moving to a 5-day delivery schedule, and resolving funding issues associated with USPS's retiree health benefits.

At the same time, USPS's 5-year plan would also reduce the overall size of the postal workforce by roughly 155,000 career employees, of which up to 35,000 would come from consolidating the mail processing network, with many of those reductions expected to result from attrition. According to the 5-year plan, half of USPS's career employees—283,000 employees—will be retirement eligible by 2016. In March 2010, USPS presented a detailed proposal to PRC to move from a 6-day to a 5-day delivery schedule to achieve its workforce and cost savings reduction goals.[24] USPS projected that its proposal to move to 5-day delivery by ending Saturday delivery would save about $3 billion annually and would reduce mail volume by less than 1 percent. However, on the basis of its review, PRC estimated a lower annual net savings—about $1.7 billion after a 3-year phase-in period—as it noted that higher revenue losses were possible.[25] In February 2012, USPS updated its projected net savings to $2.7 billion after a 3-year implementation period. Implementing 5-day delivery would require USPS to realign its operations network to increase efficiency, maintain service, and address operational issues.

Stakeholder Issues and USPS Challenges

Stakeholder Issues with Mail Processing Changes

Some business mailers have expressed concern that reducing processing facilities as a result of eliminating overnight delivery service could increase costs for business mailers who will have to travel farther to drop off their mail. In addition, business mailers have expressed concern that service could decline as USPS plans to close an unprecedented number of processing facilities in a short period. USPS employee associations have said that the proposed changes would reduce mail volume and revenue, thus making USPS's financial condition worse.

Potential Increased Costs and Service Decline for Business Mailers

Business mailers have commented that such a change in delivery service standards and postal facility locations could shift mail processing costs to them and reduce the value of mail for their businesses. While many of USPS's customers who are business mailers indicated they would be willing to accept the service standard changes and understood the need for such a change, several mailers noted that it is never good when an

---

[24]Implementing 5-day delivery would require congressional approval, since USPS's annual appropriations have required USPS to provide 6-day delivery at 1983 levels.

[25]PRC noted USPS improperly deflated mailers' reported volume decline projections and that the reported declines should not have been reduced, and determined, based on USPS's survey data, that it is likely to lose almost $600 million in net revenue because of mailer response to the proposal. See Postal Regulatory Commission, *Advisory Opinion on Elimination of Saturday Delivery*, Docket No. N2010-1 (Washington, D.C.: March 24, 2011).

organization reduces services. As a result of USPS's plan, businesses using bulk First-Class Mail, Standard Mail, or Periodicals may have fewer locations where mail can be entered and may therefore need to transport it to locations different from those now in use. Furthermore, businesses using Standard Mail may have to transport their bulk mail to other locations to take advantage of discounts. USPS officials told business mailers in February 2012, when it announced the facilities it planned to close, that it did not plan immediate changes to the locations where business mailers drop off their mail or to the associated discounts. USPS officials told us that they plan to retain business mail locations at their current locations or in close proximity.

Additionally, businesses that publish Periodicals, like daily or weekly news magazines, have expressed concern over the elimination of overnight delivery leading to deliveries not being made in a timely fashion. Delivery delays could result in customers canceling their subscriptions, thereby reducing the value of mail. These business mailers have indicated that they will most likely accelerate shifting their hard copy mail to electronic communications or otherwise stop using USPS if it is unable to provide reliable service as a result of these changes. Business mailers have also stated their concern that service could be significantly disrupted as a result of closing an unprecedented number of processing facilities by 2016. If service declines, mail users stated they are likely to lose confidence in the medium and choose to move volume and revenue from the mail to other media. Business mailers have stressed the need for USPS to put forward and share with stakeholders a comprehensive, detailed plan for consolidating its network and changes in service standards that explains to mail users what it intends to do, what changes will occur, and milestones and timelines for measuring progress in how it is achieving its plans. In sum, a key message from USPS customers is that while many support efforts to consolidate the mail processing network, it is imperative for USPS to provide consistent mail delivery and work with mailers to keep their costs down.

Employee Concern That Proposed Changes May Exacerbate Financial Problems

Employee associations have expressed concern that USPS's proposed changes may result in even greater losses in mail volume and revenue, which would further harm USPS financially. The National Association of Letter Carriers commented that downgrading service would serve only to drive customers away, reduce revenue and compromise potential growth. Further, the American Postal Workers Union and the National Rural Letter Carriers' Association commented that USPS's proposal would degrade existing USPS products, limit USPS's ability to introduce new products, place the USPS at a distinct competitive disadvantage, and severely hamper its ability to accommodate growth. USPS responded to these comments by acknowledging that its proposal would, to some degree, reduce the value of the mail to customers, but on balance is in the long-term interests of USPS to help maintain its viability for all customers into the future. USPS estimated that its proposal would result in additional volume decline of almost 2 percent, revenue decline of about $1.3 billion, with a net annual benefit of about $2 billion.

USPS Challenges to Consolidating Mail Processing

USPS faces major challenges in two areas related to consolidating its mail processing network and has told Congress that it needs legislative action to address them. Specifically, these challenges include the following:

Lack of flexibility to consolidate its workforce: USPS stated it must be able to reduce the size of its workforce in order to ensure that its costs are less than revenue. Action in this area is important since USPS's workforce accounts for about 80 percent of its costs. The Postmaster General testified last September, however, that current collective bargaining agreements prevent USPS from moving swiftly enough to achieve its planned workforce reductions. In addition, USPS has requested legislative action to eliminate the layoff protections in its collective bargaining agreements. The key challenges in this area include the following:

- *No-layoff clauses*: About 85 percent of USPS's 557,000 employees are covered by collective bargaining agreements that contain, among other provisions, employment protections such as no-layoff provisions. Currently, USPS's collective bargaining agreements with three of its major unions contain a provision stating that postal bargaining unit employees who were employed as of September 15, 1978, or, if hired after that date, have completed 6 years of continuous service are protected against any involuntary layoff or reduction in force.[26] Furthermore, USPS's memorandum of understanding with the American Postal Workers Union extends this no-layoff protection to cover those employed as of November 20, 2010—even if those employees were not otherwise eligible for no-layoff protection. The collective bargaining agreement with its fourth major union—the

---

[26]USPS's labor force is primarily represented by the American Postal Workers Union (about 222,000 members), National Association of Letter Carriers (about 286,000 members), National Postal Mail Handlers Union (about 50,000 members), and National Rural Letter Carriers' Association (about 110,000 members).

National Rural Letter Carriers' Association—states that that no bargaining unit employees employed in the career workforce will be laid off on an involuntary basis during the period of the agreement. The no-layoff clauses will be a challenge to USPS primarily if it cannot achieve its workforce reductions through attrition. With the large number of employees eligible for retirement, USPS has a window of opportunity to avoid layoffs of non-bargaining unit employees who are not eligible for no-layoff protection.

- *Fifty-mile limits on employee transfers:* In 2011, the American Postal Workers Union (which represents USPS clerks, maintenance employees, and motor vehicle service workers) and USPS management negotiated a 4-year agreement that limits transferring employees of an installation or craft to no more than 50 miles away. If USPS management cannot place employees within 50 miles, the parties are to jointly determine what steps may be taken, which includes putting postal employees on "standby," which occurs when workers are idled but paid their full salary because of reassignments and reorganization efforts. USPS may face challenges in capturing cost savings as a result of its initiatives to reduce excess capacity because of its limited ability to move mail processing clerks from a facility where workloads no longer support the number of clerk positions needed to facilities with vacant positions.

Collective bargaining agreements have expired for three of the four major postal unions, and because of impasses in negotiations, USPS has moved to arbitration with these unions. In 2011, USPS reported that it had no assurance that it would be able to negotiate collective bargaining agreements with its unions that would result in a cost structure that is sustainable within current and projected future mail revenue levels. It noted that there is no current mandate requiring an arbitrator to consider the financial health of USPS in its decision and an unfavorable arbitration decision could have significant adverse consequences on its ability to meet future financial obligations.

Resistance to facility closures: USPS is facing resistance to its plans to consolidate or close postal facilities from Members of Congress, affected communities, and its employees and has requested congressional action to enable it to consolidate and close facilities. We reviewed numerous comments from Members of Congress, affected communities, and employee organizations that have expressed opposition to closing facilities. Such concerns are particularly heightened for postal facilities identified for closure that may consolidate functions to another state, causing political leaders to oppose and potentially prevent such consolidations. For example, Members of Congress have resisted a recent proposal to move certain processing functions from its Rockford, Illinois, Processing and Distribution Center to a processing facility in Madison, Wisconsin. This proposal would eliminate the need for 82 employees (77 bargaining unit and 5 management staff) in Rockford that USPS would need to transfer into new roles or to another facility. The president of the Springfield Chamber of Commerce sent a letter to PRC to protest USPS's planned consolidation of the Springfield, Illinois, processing facility into St. Louis, Missouri, stating that this move would reduce service quality and increase costs, affecting its members' profitability and operations. He added that Springfield would lose up to 300 jobs in an area of the community that qualifies as an "Area of Greatest Need," according to the U.S. Department of Housing and Urban Development.

In contrast, however, other business mailers and Members of Congress have expressed support for consolidating the mail processing network to reduce costs. Some business mailers have stated that USPS needs to take cost-saving action to reduce the need for significant postal rate increases. A significant postal increase would have a detrimental financial impact on mailers by decreasing mail's return on investment and may also accelerate mailers' shift toward electronic communication. In addition, as we discuss below, some Members of Congress have proposed legislation supporting USPS efforts to consolidate its mail processing network.

Other stakeholders, including USPS's employee associations, have questioned whether USPS needs to make drastic changes by reducing service and the size of its networks and workforce, since they believe that USPS's financial crisis is, at least in part, artificial. They point out that most of USPS's losses since fiscal year 2006 are due to the requirement to prefund its future retiree health benefits. In 2006, PAEA established a 10-year schedule of USPS payments into a fund (the Postal Service Retiree Health Benefits Fund) that averaged $5.6 billion per year through fiscal year 2016.[27] Employee associations have stated that such a requirement is exceptional and unfair, since no other federal agency is forced to prefund its employees' health benefits at this level and no company has such a mandate. They have suggested that instead of reducing costs, Congress should eliminate the prefunding requirements, return surpluses in its retirement accounts, and

---

[27]Pub. L. No. 109-435, § 803(a).

allow USPS to earn additional revenue by offering new services. USPS responded that given the multibillion-dollar deficits that it has experienced in each of the last 5 years, and given the over $14 billion loss it expects in fiscal year 2012, capturing cost savings wherever possible will be vital to USPS's financial viability.

If USPS cannot increase revenues enough to eliminate its net losses, it will have to do more to reduce costs. To address USPS prefunding issues, we testified that deferring some prefunding of USPS's retiree health benefits would serve as short-term fiscal relief. However, deferrals also increase the risk that USPS will not be able to make future payments as its core business declines. Therefore, we concluded that it is important for USPS to continue funding its retiree health benefit obligations—including prefunding these obligations—to the maximum extent that its finances permit.[28]

Pending Legislation to Address USPS Challenges

USPS has stated that it needs action from Congress to address restrictions that limit its ability to consolidate its mail processing network, including annual appropriations provisions that mandate 6-day delivery,[29] and granting USPS authority to determine delivery frequency. Some Members have asked USPS to postpone actions to consolidate mail processing facilities so it would not preempt Congress on postal reform. In response to the Members' request, USPS agreed last December to place a moratorium on closing facilities until May 15, 2012.

As of April 2012, the House of Representatives and Senate committees with USPS oversight responsibility have passed bills to help USPS achieve financial viability. These bills, as well as other postal reform bills, include provisions that could affect USPS's ability to consolidate its mail processing network. Table 4 summarizes the key provisions of the House of Representatives bill—H.R. 2309, the Postal Reform Act of 2011—and Senate bill—S. 1789, the 21st Century Postal Service Act.

---

[28]GAO-11-926T.

[29]These provisions have specified that "6-day delivery and rural delivery of mail shall continue at not less than the 1983 level." See e.g., Pub. L. No. 112-74, 125 Stat. 786.

Table 4: Summary of Key Pending Legislation Related to Optimizing Mail Processing Network

Pending legislation	Legislative provisions on USPS processing network optimization effort
21st Century Postal Service Act, S. 1789, 112th Cong. (2011)	• Requires USPS to complete a study prior to the closure of a processing facility, which evaluates the option of downsizing rather than closing the facility.
	• Prohibits USPS from implementing its plan to eliminate Saturday delivery for at least 2 years. The implementation could move forward only if certain conditions are met, including developing remedies for affected customers, making full use of its authority to increase revenue and reduce costs, and requiring GAO to evaluate the financial need for such change.
	• Requires that arbitrators deciding a contract dispute between USPS and its labor organizations take into consideration USPS's financial condition, among other considerations.
	• Authorizes use of surplus funding from retirement accounts to offer buyouts of up to $25,000 for eligible employees.
Postal Reform Act of 2011, H.R. 2309, 112th Cong. (2011)	• Creates the Commission on Postal Reorganization, which would be tasked with recommending facility closures.
	• Requires USPS to develop and submit a plan to the Commission on Postal Reorganization for the closure of mail processing and other facilities and offices. Requires the commission to transmit the plan to Congress, publish the report containing the commission's findings in the *Federal Register,* and hold public hearings. Requires USPS to implement the closure or consolidation of postal facilities and offices recommended by the commission unless Congress enacts a joint resolution disapproving the commission's recommendations.
	• Authorizes USPS to declare up to 12 non-mail delivery days annually so long as it is required to deliver mail 6 days per week.[a]
	• Reforms the collective bargaining process to contain a mediation-arbitration process. Requires any arbitration decision to take into account both pay comparability with the private sector and USPS's financial condition. Prohibits collective bargaining agreements from containing provisions that restrict the use of reduction-in-force procedures, which could include no-layoff clauses.

Source: GAO analysis.

[a]Within 6 months of enactment, USPS would be allowed to submit a proposal to move to a 5-day delivery schedule and can implement such a delivery schedule 90 days after PRC renders an advisory opinion, notwithstanding any other provision of law.

Pending legislation originating in the Senate (S.1789) includes provisions that would affect USPS's ability to consolidate its networks by delaying USPS's move to 5-day delivery by 2 years and requiring USPS to consider downsizing rather than closing facilities. Delaying USPS's move to a 5-day delivery schedule could make it difficult for USPS to save $22.5 billion by 2016. On the other hand, the Senate bill includes a requirement for arbitrators to consider USPS's financial condition and could facilitate attrition by allowing USPS to use surplus pension funds to pay for employee buyouts of up to $25,000 for as many as 100,000 eligible postal workers. Such buyouts may make it easier to reduce USPS's workforce in facilities targeted for closure.

Another legislative proposal, originating in the House of Representatives, (H.R. 2309) includes provisions that would enhance USPS's ability to consolidate its mail processing network by allowing changes in service standards and using a BRAC framework to approve a consolidation plan, address some of the political resistance to closing postal facilities, and potentially reform the collective bargaining process. The proposed Commission on Postal Reorganization could broaden the current focus on individual facility closures—which are often contentious, time–consuming, and inefficient—to a broader networkwide restructuring, similar to the BRAC approach. In other restructuring efforts where this approach has been used, expert panels have successfully informed and permitted difficult restructuring decisions, helping to provide consensus on intractable decisions. As previously noted, the 2003 Report of the President's Commission on the USPS also recommended such an approach relating to the consolidation and rationalization of USPS's mail processing and distribution infrastructure. We also reported in 2010 that Congress may want to consider this approach to assist in restructuring organizations that are facing key financial challenges.[30] In addition, the House bill authorizes USPS to declare up to 12 non-mail delivery days annually so long as USPS is required to deliver mail 6 days per week and reforms the collective bargaining process, including requiring arbitrators to consider USPS's financial condition.

Concluding Observations

Developing an optimal mail processing network will require both congressional support and USPS leadership. Moreover, we have previously reported that Congress and USPS need to reach agreement on a comprehensive package of actions to improve USPS's financial viability. In these previous reports, we provided strategies and options

---

[30]GAO-10-455.

that Congress could consider to better align USPS costs with revenues and address constraints and legal restrictions that limit USPS's ability to reduce costs and improve efficiency. Consequently, we are not making new recommendations or presenting a matter for Congress to consider at this time. Without congressional action to help USPS address its financial problems, USPS will be limited in the amount of rate increase it may seek and may fall even further into debt. USPS had $2 billion remaining on its $15 billion statutory borrowing limit at the end of fiscal year 2011. It is now abundantly clear that the postal business model must be fixed given the dramatic and estimated decline in volume, particularly for First-Class Mail. If Congress prefers to retain the current delivery service standards and associated network, decisions will be needed about how USPS's costs for providing these services will be paid, including additional cost reductions or revenue sources.

Agency Comments

We provided a draft of this report to USPS for review and comment. USPS had no comments, but provided technical clarifications, which we incorporated into the report as appropriate.

We are sending copies of this report to the appropriate congressional committees, the Postmaster General, and other interested parties. In addition, the report is available at no charge on GAO's website at http://www.gao.gov.

If you or your staff have any questions on this report, please contact me at (202) 512-2834 or stjamesl@gao.gov. Contact points for our Offices of Congressional Relations and Public Affairs may be found on the last page of this report. Contact information and key contributors to the report are listed in appendix II.

Lorelei St. James
Director
Physical Infrastructure Issues

Appendix I: Objectives, Scope, and Methodology

This report addresses (1) past actions the U.S. Postal Service (USPS) has taken to reduce excess capacity, (2) USPS's plans to consolidate its mail processing network, and (3) key stakeholder issues and challenges USPS faces in consolidating its mail processing network.

To describe what actions USPS has taken to reduce excess capacity, we obtained data from USPS related to changes in its mail processing network, workforce, and costs as well as an updated 10-year volume forecast for First-Class Mail. To calculate the 5-year cost savings that USPS achieved, we took the difference of the network costs for fiscal years 2006 and 2011 that USPS reported to us. We also obtained data from USPS and USPS Office of Inspector General (OIG) reports regarding cost savings related to USPS initiatives to reduce excess capacity. Further, we reviewed USPS annual reports to Congress and its network plans as section 302 of the Postal Accountability and Enhancement Act of 2006 requires USPS to submit; related GAO and USPS OIG reports, as well as other relevant studies relating to reducing excess capacity in USPS's mail processing network.

To examine USPS's future plans to consolidate its mail processing network, we reviewed USPS's December 2011 proposal to change delivery service standards and its plan to consolidate its mail processing network by reducing facilities, staff, equipment, and transportation resources. We also reviewed USPS's 5-year business plan to profitability issued in February 2012. We interviewed USPS senior management and local facility mangers in Illinois about the current processing network and future plans for that network. We also reviewed documents in the ongoing Postal Regulatory Commission (PRC) review of USPS's proposed changes in service standards and its plan for consolidating its mail processing network. PRC is reviewing USPS's estimated cost savings, service impacts, and public input on the proposed service standard changes and expects to complete its review sometime after July 2012.

To determine key issues and challenges USPS faces in consolidating its mail processing network, we reviewed and summarized concerns from postal stakeholders responding to the USPS's September 2011 *Federal Register* notice on its proposed changes to service standards for First-Class Mail, Periodicals, and Standard Mail. We also interviewed USPS officials, and reviewed stakeholder testimonies and published letters from Members of Congress commenting on USPS plans to change delivery service standards and close facilities. We further reviewed pending legislative proposals that could affect USPS's efforts to address excess capacity and consolidate its mail processing network.

We conducted this performance audit from April 2011 through April 2012 in accordance with generally accepted government auditing standards. Those standards require that we plan and perform the audit to obtain sufficient, appropriate evidence to provide a reasonable basis for our findings and conclusions based on our audit objectives. We believe that the evidence obtained provides a reasonable basis for our findings and conclusions based on our audit objectives.

Appendix II: GAO Contact and Staff Acknowledgments

GAO Contact	Lorelei St. James, (202) 512-2834 or stjamesl@gao.gov
Staff Acknowledgments	In addition to the individual named above, Teresa Anderson (Assistant Director), Samer Abbas, Joshua Bartzen, Erin R. Cohen, Sara Ann Moessbauer, Amy Rosewarne, and Crystal Wesco made key contributions to this report.

GAO's Mission	The Government Accountability Office, the audit, evaluation, and investigative arm of Congress, exists to support Congress in meeting its constitutional responsibilities and to help improve the performance and accountability of the federal government for the American people. GAO examines the use of public funds; evaluates federal programs and policies; and provides analyses, recommendations, and other assistance to help Congress make informed oversight, policy, and funding decisions. GAO's commitment to good government is reflected in its core values of accountability, integrity, and reliability.
Obtaining Copies of GAO Reports and Testimony	The fastest and easiest way to obtain copies of GAO documents at no cost is through GAO's website (www.gao.gov). Each weekday afternoon, GAO posts on its website newly released reports, testimony, and correspondence. To have GAO e-mail you a list of newly posted products, go to www.gao.gov and select "E-mail Updates."
Order by Phone	The price of each GAO publication reflects GAO's actual cost of production and distribution and depends on the number of pages in the publication and whether the publication is printed in color or black and white. Pricing and ordering information is posted on GAO's website, http://www.gao.gov/ordering.htm. Place orders by calling (202) 512-6000, toll free (866) 801-7077, or TDD (202) 512-2537. Orders may be paid for using American Express, Discover Card, MasterCard, Visa, check, or money order. Call for additional information.
Connect with GAO	Connect with GAO on Facebook, Flickr, Twitter, and YouTube. Subscribe to our RSS Feeds or E-mail Updates. Listen to our Podcasts. Visit GAO on the web at www.gao.gov.
To Report Fraud, Waste, and Abuse in Federal Programs	Contact: Website: www.gao.gov/fraudnet/fraudnet.htm E-mail: fraudnet@gao.gov Automated answering system: (800) 424-5454 or (202) 512-7470
Congressional Relations	Katherine Siggerud, Managing Director, siggerudk@gao.gov, (202) 512-4400, U.S. Government Accountability Office, 441 G Street NW, Room 7125, Washington, DC 20548
Public Affairs	Chuck Young, Managing Director, youngc1@gao.gov, (202) 512-4800 U.S. Government Accountability Office, 441 G Street NW, Room 7149 Washington, DC 20548

Please Print on Recycled Paper.

www.ingramcontent.com/pod-product-compliance
Lightning Source LLC
Chambersburg PA
CBHW080937290526
45795CB00007BA/2797